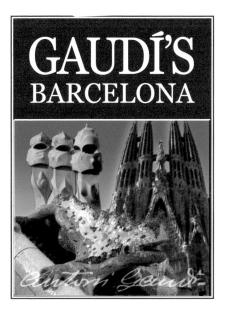

GAUDÍ'S
BARCELONA

Núria Casas / Lourdes Mateo

Pòrtic Guies

gaudí 2**0**02 Barcelona
Any Internacional Gaudí
Año Internacional Gaudí
Gaudí International Year
Année Internationale Gaudí

The authors express their thanks to historian Pilar Mateo Bretos for her collaboration in editing the cronology.

PUBLISHING DIRECTOR
Jesús Giralt

PÒRTIC DIRECTOR
Francesc Boada

EDITORIAL
Anna Pérez i Mir and Xavier de Juan

DESIGN AND LAYOUT
Domènec Òrrit
based on an idea by the authors

PHOTOGRAPHY
Salvador Redó
Joaquim Camp
Luís Gueilburt
Arxiu fotogràfic del CEC
ECSA
ECSA-Arxiu Mas
ECSA-BC
ECSA-D. Casanova
ECSA-Gabriel Serra
ECSA-IMH
ECSA-Maspons Ubiña
ECSA-Pere Virgili
ECSA-Rambol
Index
Institut Ametller d'Art Hispànic
Prisma
Tavisa

Translated by:
Andrew Stacey

FIRST PUBLISHED : juliol del 2001
© text: Núria Casas Soler and
   Lourdes Mateo Bretos, 2001

ALL RIGHTS TO THIS PUBLICATION:
ECSA, Diputació, 250 - 08007 Barcelona
www.editorial-portic.com
portic@grec.com

PHOTOMECANICAL PROCESS: Marquès, S.L.
PRINTED BY: Tallers Gràfics Soler. Enric Morera, 15
Esplugues de Llobregat

ISBN: 84-7306-681-2
Legal Diposit: B.27049-2001

TABLE OF CONTENTS

INTRODUCTION

The guide book **Gaudí's Barcelona** is intended to be a new and up-to-date way of learning about the work of the famous Catalan architect, Antoni Gaudí.

Following the trends set by new technologies, books in the field of cultural information are incorporating more and more attractive pedagogical illustrations which convey the message more easily. Likewise, in recent times guidebook publications have undergone a considerable change in this respect.

Therefore our guidebook intends, along these modern lines, to point out the necessary elements in order to learn about Gaudí and his work. However, it goes one step further, and without forgetting its function as a guidebook —as the very name indicates— wishes to "accompany" the visitor during his or her visit to the wonderful world of Gaudí's architecture. For this reason, **Gaudí's Barcelona** "dissects" the building, guides the visitor, acompanies them on their way, suggests details that may be observed, and which might otherwise go unnoticed... Finally, in a neutral and objective way, it enables the visitor to make a personal value judgement on Gaudí's admirable work.

This book covers the buildings constructed by the architect in Barcelona, both city and province, in fourteen chapters. A brief reference to his work in the rest of Spain is also included. A complete chronology will permit us to place his work in the historical context of the time. Lastly, there is a glossary to help us to understand the more specialized architectural terminology.

ANTONI GAUDÍ: HIS WORK

The work of the architect Antoni Gaudí is inseparable from Barcelona. An inventor of forms, he developed a very personal body of work that kept him related only tangentially to the artistic vanguard, turning his buildings into architectural landmarks. His works are the attempt to seek reality through geometry, shapes he obtained through observing nature itself, as in the case of parabolic arches, his favourite shape, perfectly reflected in the form of the trees. It is also relevant how in his work he captures the marriage between ornamentation and structure that eventually becomes indissoluble. In this way, the decorative elements often perform structural functions and viceversa.

During his student days he worked with architects who transmitted to him a taste for historicist styles. Thus, working with Joan Martorell or the master builder Josep Fontseré i Mestre, Gaudí became interested in Gothic and Mudéjar styles —the Güell Pavilions, Park Güell— and impregnated his architecture with a deep symbolism gleaned from various sources: religious symbols, natural forms, mediaeval heraldry... He maintained this eclecticism until about 1900; from that time on until 1917 he enjoyed his most creative and innovative period —carrying out his most characteristic works— Casa Batlló, Casa Milà or the Park Güell. It is in this period when he is linked to Modernism; a relationship which cannot be denied, but which it is necessary to qualify, as Gaudí often took up a reactionary stance towards the progressive movements represented by Modernism, and aesthetically he went beyond its limits. From then until his death, Gaudí lived only for the Sagrada Família, the culmination of his geometric and symbolic quest.

This controversial fugure has generated an abundant bibliography and analyses with quite contrasting criteria. Thus, the study of his work has shown Gaudí either as the creator of a new style of architecture or as the last word in the 19th monumental tradition. Regardless of the stance taken, we cannot overlook the Sagrada Família as the reflection of the trends inherited from the 19th from the ideological and architectonic point of view, not so much for the structural innovation as for the building's monumentality.

	Gaudí: his life and works	Historical events	Architectural works
1851			The Crystal Palace, by J. Paxton, built on the occasion of the Great Exhibition in London.
1852	Antoni Gaudí i Cornet, son of Francesc Gaudí i Serra and Antònia Cornet i Bertran, is born in Reus on June 25th.	Louis Napoleon Bonaparte proclaimed Emperor as Napoleon III. / The Transvaal Free State founded in South Africa by the Boers.	Pavilion Richelieu, Paris, by Louis Visconti.
1855		Alexander II crowned Tsar of Russia.	
1856		Crimean War ends with the Treaty of Paris. / Cranium of "Neanderthal Man" found.	
1859		*"The Origin of the Species" by Charles Darwin.*	The planner Ildefons Cerdà publishes his *Proyecto de Reforma y Ensanche de la ciudad de Barcelona.*
1861			Start of the Paris Opera House by Charles Garnier.
1863	Gaudí receives religious teaching during his Bachillerato studies in the Escolapis school in Reus.		Start of building work on the University building in Barcelona, by Elias Rogent.
1864		The International Workers' Association (First International) founded, of which Karl Marx is a member.	
1865		End of American Civil War and assassination of Abraham Lincoln, President of the USA.	
1867		Otto von Bismark, Chancellor of the North German Federation. / Karl Marx publishes Das Kapital.	
1868			Start of building in iron of the National Library in Paris, by the architect Henri Labrouste.
1870		End of the Second Napoleonic Empire in France.	Brooklyn Bridge, New York, by J. Roebling.
1871			Opening of the Albert Hall in London.
1872		Monet paints "Impression: Sunrise", from whose title the term Impressionism is coined to refer to an artistic movement.	
1873	He studies architecture at the Escola Provincial d'Arquitectura in Barcelona. As a student, he takes part in some projects: a topographic map of the build- ing site marked out for the *Diputació de Barcelona*; as a draughtsman he takes part in work in the Ciutadella Park, the Monastery of Montserrat, the plan for the fountain in Plaça de Catalunya, and so on.	The First Spanish Republic is proclaimed.	Palmer House Hotel, Chicago, by John M. van Odsel.
1875		End of the Spanish Republic, restoration of the monarchy and coronation of Alfonso XII as King of Spain.	
1876	His mother, Antònia Cornet, dies.	In Catalonia the flourishing period known as "El Febre d'Or" (Gold Fever) begins.	Building of the Sacred Heart Basilica in Montmartre, Paris. / Bon Marché depart ment store Paris, by L.A. Boileau and Gustave Eiffel.

	Gaudí: his life and works	Historical events	Architectural works
1878	He receives the title of architect and sets up professionally in Carrer del Call in Barcelona.		Sever Hall, Cambridge (USA), by Henry Hobson Richardson.
1879	He carries out several projects (lampposts for the city of Barcelona, commercial	Pablo Iglesias founds the Spanish Socialist Workers' Party (PSOE).	Leiter building, Chicago, by W. Le Baron Jenney.
1880	establishments, furniture and liturgical objects, pavilions and furniture for private clients,	The Republic of South Africa proclaimed in the Transvaal.	
1881	etc). He helps the architect Joan Martorell on the project for two	The painter Pablo Ruiz Picasso born.	
1882	churches in Barcelona. The start of Casa Vicens, in Carrer de les Carolines in Barcelona.	Robert Koch discovers the tuberculosis bacillum.	Viaducto del Garabit, by the Frenchman Gustave Eiffel, in Barcelona. / Project for Ciudad Lineal, Madrid, by Arturo Soria y Mata.
1883	The construction of the villa El Capricho, in Santander. / He figures for the first time as	The philosopher Karl Marx and the composer Richard Wagner die.	
1884	the architect in charge of the work on the Sagrada Família, in Barcelona. / His name is on the project for the Chapel of Saint Joseph in the apse of the crypt under the Sagrada Família.	The term Modernist appears for the first time in Catalonia, later to be applied to the artistic movement.	Reichstag building, Berlin, by P. Wallot.
1886	The start of the Güell Palace, in Barcelona, for Eusebi Güell.	*Beyond Good and Evil by F.W. Nietzsche. / The Statue of Liberty, by the Frenchman Frédéric-Auguste Bartholdi, is erected in New York.*	La Bourse, Paris, by Henri Blondel. / Tower Bridge, London, by Horace Jones. / Auditorium Building, Chicago, by Louis H. Sullivan.
1887	The start of the Episcopal Palace in Astorga, León.		The Catalan Modernist architect Lluís Domènech i Montaner builds the Ateneu in Canet de Mar (Barcelona). / Start of the Eiffel Tower in Paris by Gustave Eiffel.
1888	The Compañía Transatlántica's pavilion at the Barcelona Universal Exhibition.	The Peral submarine, invented by the scientist Isaac Peral, is presented. / "The Bedroom at Arles" by Vincent van Gogh. / First Universal Exhibition in Barcelona.	The Columbus monument in Barcelona by Gaietà Buïgas. Arc del Triomf de Barcelona, by Josep Vilaseca, for the Universal Exhibition.
1889	1889-1895: Several projects for private clients and religious institutions.	The Worker's Festival first held on May 1st.	The Machine Gallery, by the architect C.L.F. Dutert, built, for the International Exhibition in Paris.
1890	Crypt and part of the apse of the temple of the Sagrada Família.	The artistic movement Art Nouveau begins.	Project by the architect Otto Wagner to reurbanise the city of Vienna.
1892		The Coca-Cola company founded in Atlanta.	
1893		The painter Joan Miró born. / The Scream, by Edvard Munch. / A bomb explodes in the Liceu, Barcelona.	Tassel House, Brussels, by the Belgian architect Victor Horta.

	Gaudí: his life and works	Historical events	Architectural works
1894		Nicholas II accedes to the Russian throne.	
1896		Presentation of the cinematograph in Paris, by the Lumière brothers. / The first modern Olympic Games held in Athens.	
1897			Glasgow School of Art, by the architect Charles Renni Mackintosh.
1898	Casa Calvet, in Carrer de Casp, Barcelona. Beginning of the project for the church at the Güell Industrial village, in Santa Coloma de Cervelló.	After the Spanish-American war, Spain gives up Cuba and gives Puerto Rico and the Philippines to the U.S.A. / Pierre and Marie Curie separate polonium and radium from uranium.	Exhibition building for the Vienna Secession, by the Austrian Josef Maria Olbrich.
1899		The Boer War in South Africa. / The German chemist Bayer produces aspirin.	Maison du Peuple, Brussels by Victor Horta.
1900	He receives a prize for Casa Calvet from Barcelona City Council. Casa Bellesguard, in Barcelona. / The start of the Parc Güell, Barcelona, commissioned by its developer, Eusebi Güell. "Christ's Resurrection" for the Monumental Rosary of Montserrat.	S. Freud publishes *The Interpretation of Dreams.* / The German F. von Zeppelin builds his first dirigible.	Casa Amatller, by J. Puig i Cadafalch. / Entrances to the Paris Metro, by H. Guimard.
1901	The gate and perimeter wall of the printer Hermengild Miralles' estate in Passeig de Manuel Girona, Barcelona.	Marconi invents the radio. Theodore Roosevelt, President of the USA.	
1902		Alfonso XIII, King of Spain. / W.S. Sutton points out the hereditary character of chromosomes.	Apartment block in rue Franklin, Paris, by the French architect Auguste Perret.
1903	The start of the restoration work on Mallorca Cathedral.	The Wright brothers make the first manned flight in an aeroplane in North Carolina, USA.	Postal Savings Bank, Vienna, by Otto Wagner.
1904	Casa Batlló, in Passeig de Gràcia, Barcelona, for Josep Batlló.		Carson Pirie Scott store, by Louis Henry Sullivan, founder of the Chicago school.
1905	Francesc Berenguer builds a house in the Parc Güell which was later to become Gaudí's home until his death, and which was later turned into the Casa Museu Gaudí in 1963.	The Theory of Relativity by Albert Einstein.	Start of the Palau de la Música Catalana, by Lluís Domènech i Montaner.
1906	His father, Francesc Gaudí, dies. / Casa Milà, "La Pedrera", in Passeig de Gràcia, Barcelona, for Pere Milà.		
1907		"Les Demoiselles d'Avignon" by Picasso.	Robie house, Chicago, by Frank Lloyd Wright.
1908	The crypt at the Güell industrial village, in Santa Coloma de Cervelló.	Mass production begins on the Ford Model T automobile.	Coonley house, Riverside (USA), by Frank Lloyd Wright.
1909		R.E.Peary reaches the North Pole.	

	Gaudí: his life and works	Historical events	Architectural works
1910	The Gaudí Exhibition is held in Paris on the occasion of the 1910 Salon, organized by the "Société Nationale des Beaux-Arts".		Fagus Works, Alfeld, Germany, by Walter Gropius and Adolph Mayer. / Steiner house, Vienna, by Adolf Loos.
1911		R.E.Amundsen reaches the South Pole.	Stoclet House, Brussels, by Josef Hoffmann.
1914		Start of the First World War. / Ghandi returns to India to combat British rule.	Domino housing project by Le Corbusier.
1916			Start of the Imperial Hotel in Tokyo, by F.L. Wright.
1917		Russian Revolution.	
1918		End of the First World War. / Czechoslovakia and Yugoslavia founded. / Creation of the Weimar Republic in Germany.	
1919		Treaty of Versailles, signed at the end of the First World War between Germany and the victorious allied powers. / Artistic movement Noucentisme in Catalonia.	Foundation of the Bauhaus school in Weimar by the architect Walter Gropius.
1920			Einstein Observatory, Potsdam, by E. Mendelsohn.
1921		The Irish Free State is recognized.	
1922		After the "March on Rome", Mussolini forms a government. / The Union of Soviet Socialist Republics (USSR) is formed.	
1923		General Primo de Rivera's coup d'état in Spain. / Invention of the autogyro by J. de la Cierva.	
1924		Death of Lenin on January 21st. / A cranium later known as belonging to the genus *Australopithecus* is found in South Africa..	The Working Men's Club, Jyväskylä, Finland, by Alvar Aalto.
1925	He devotes himself mainly to the work on the Sagrada Família.	The first part of Hitler's *Mein Kampf* published. / Treaties of Locarno, signed to strengthen security in Western Europe after the First World War.	Bauhaus buildings in Dessau, by W. Gropius. / Esprit Nouveau Pavilion, Paris, by Le Corbusier.
1926	Gaudí is knocked down by a tramcar in Barcelona, dying a few days later.	Hirohito ascends the throne as Emperor of Japan, succeeding his father, Yoshihito.	

Lampposts

in
Plaça Reial
and Pla de Palau

1878

T he lampposts, in both Plaça Reial and Pla de Palau formed part of urban renovation projects carried out in the 19th century. Plaça Reial, enclosed by uniform buildings with a colonnaded ground floor, was developed according to Francesc Daniel i Molina's plan after the demolition of the monastery on the site, occupied by Capuchin monks since 1718. El Pla de Palau also has its origin in a nineteenth-century plan, drawn up by Colonel Josep Massanés in 1820, which created an open space flanked by the Llotja (stock exchange), the Customs House —now the Delegació del Govern— and the Viceroys' Palace, since destroyed by fire. The square was enlarged in 1833 after the demolition of the sea wall, and the monumental Portal del Mar was built, although this is no longer standing. A few years later the Porxos d'en Xifré and Casa Collasso were built, plus the El Geni Català fountain and, much later, in 1930-33, the Faculty of Nautical Studies gave the square its present appearance.

| **Metro** Liceu, Barceloneta, Jaume I. | **Buses** 14, 17, 19, 38, 40, 45, 57, 59, 64, 100, 157 | **Open to the public** |

I n 1878 Gaudí was commissioned by Barcelona City Council to design some gas lampposts —*candelabra* is the world used in the project minutes— for Plaça Reial, an area of great distinction at that time, to be lit during the festivals of La Mercè in 1879. He was also commissioned to design four more lampposts of the same model but simpler: two for El Pla de Palau and two more, which have since disappeared, to be set at the entrance to La Barceloneta. In the job he was aided by several craftsmen, including the Valls Hermanos foundry and the glassmaker Eudald Ramon Amigó.

The caduceus (a staff twined with serpents) and winged helmet are the symbols of Mercury, the Roman god of commerce, the activity most representative of the city. With this, Gaudí tried to express the historical Barcelona looking forward to the future. The material used was cast iron, except at the base of the column, where he used polished marble.

The arms of Barcelona appear on the shaft of the column.

Plaça Reial

The surprising colours —blue, red, gold — that we can see were restored very recently, in 2000, after disappearing on several occasions, the last as a result of alterations to the square in 1983, when the lampposts were painted black.

Gaudí justified the use of six arms on the lampposts, because, situated at the same height, they gave an even light.

He claimed that such an effect was possible with three, five and numbers above six.

However, the four-armed cross shape was not considered suitable.

These lampposts were restored to their original colours at the end of the 1990s.

Pla de Palau

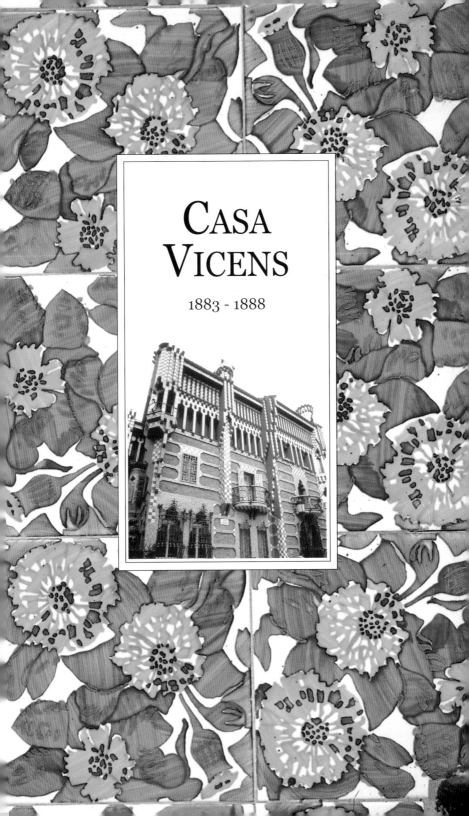

CASA
VICENS

1883 - 1888

Casa Vicens is in the popular district of Gràcia, which grew up in the 17th and 18th centuries when country estates like La Fontana and Can Trilla were built there. The name Gràcia appears in the records for the year 1767 referring to a fully consolidated urban centre. These days it is full of small cafés, restaurants, cinemas and theatres, and has become one of the liveliest centres of Barcelona's nightlife. Its narrow streets keep alive the memory of the old "Town of Gràcia", which in the 19th century underwent the change from a rural to an industrial society. In 1897, this important town was annexed to Barcelona along with other surrounding towns and villages.

Carrer de les Carolines, 18-24	**Metro** Fontana	**Buses** 22, 24, 26, 28	**Not open to the public**

G audí planned this summer family house, commissioned by Manuel Vicens Montaner, in 1878, building it between 1883 and 1888. It belongs to Gaudí's early period in which inspiration from history, Mediterranean roots and Oriental style predominate.

Although structurally speaking it added nothing new, this early work by Gaudí was significant in the eclectic European currents at the end of the 19th century. Its most characteristic feature was its expressive strength, fruit of a complex distribution of space and profuse decoration for which Gaudí used generous amounts of tiling.

Initially the house only occupied a small site. It was a very simple construction, developed from two single parallel spaces, and attached at the back to a dividing wall belonging to a nunnery. It comprised a lower ground floor for store rooms, a box-room and a kitchen, a ground floor with a living-dining room, a smoking room, a hall and two other rooms, a first floor with the family's bedrooms and a second floor with the servants' quarters. In front of the house was a small garden.

In 1925, as it was by now being used as a permanent residence, the house underwent an enlargement scheme designed by Juan Bautista Serra de Martínez and approved by Gaudí. An extension was added onto the existing structure and the doorways were changed whilst maintaining the stylistic unity of the building. The garden was enlarged by the addition of a further plot of land and a domed chapel dedicated to Saint Rita was erected in the part furthest from the house. In 1927 it was awarded the City Council's prize for the best building in the city.

The building comprises three **façades** enveloped in a continuous series of skilfully intermingled corporeal elements, geometric and polychrome shapes, which clearly show the architect's creative imagination.

Corner gallery with a

balcony

resting on long brick corbels.

Terracotta figures of children by the sculptor Riba y García (1859-1932) on the parapets of the balconies.

Central **gallery**, originally enclosed by wooden latticework opening outwards on hinges and featuring ornamentation of Far Eastern inspiration. It was altered in 1925 with the incorporation of a large window. Gaudí added some words to the frieze on the gallery alluding to the house's orientation towards the sun.

Towards the northwest, *"Oh, la sombra del verano"* (Oh, the shadow of summer),
to the southeast, *"Sol, solecito, ven a verme"* (Sun, please come and see me)
and to the southwest where the chimney is, *"Del hogar el fuego, viva el juego de amor"* (From the hearth comes fire, long live the game of love).

On the lower floors the **wall** of the building is of exposed masonry combined with horizontal ribbons of brick and covered with decorated ceramic.

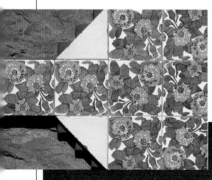

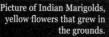

Picture of Indian Marigolds, yellow flowers that grew in the grounds.

Very thin brick pillars, which split into two as they rise.

Gazebo with ceramic decoration

The **upper floor**

features vertical forms with a great lightness of volume and ceramic decoration in a green and white draughtboard pattern.

The **roof**

is of brick tiles on sloping wooden beams. On the rooftop, of Arab tiles, a walkway goes round the edge of the house giving the idea of a castle. In the highest parts, gazebos —crowned by polychrome cupolas and fitted with benches to sit on— give a nice view of the garden.

Chimney

with a polygonal stack and circular pot on top, covered with green and white glazed ceramic tiles. It runs strategically up the central part of the front wall, appearing as part of the ornamentation. As is usual with Gaudí, there is a symbiosis between decoration and function.

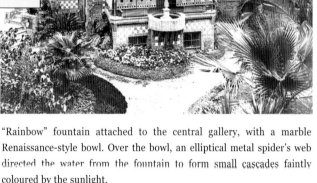

The **garden** was designed in close harmony with the building in order to optimize contact with nature. Over time, most of its significant elements have been lost or modified due to the alterations to the house in 1925 and the urban development around the site.

The house and garden as they looked originally.

"Rainbow" fountain attached to the central gallery, with a marble Renaissance-style bowl. Over the bowl, an elliptical metal spider's web directed the water from the fountain to form small cascades faintly coloured by the sunlight.

Monumental waterfall built onto the end wall of the garden. It was made of brick and featured a parabolic arch that could be crossed by a covered path and steps at either side, a bowl and grotto where the water flowed.

The gate's present appearance dates
back to the alterations of 1925-27.

With the alterations, access to the
house from the garden was changed;
the staircase disappeared, the left
side arch of the portico was turned
into the new front door and the others
into windows.

Gaudí put all his ingenuity into the
small details, including them in his
architectural plan. This can be seen in
the artistic treatment of the **gate**,
featuring a palmetto (or Margallon
palm) leaf made in cast-iron by Joan
Oñós, seen in the photograph, whose
model was originally designed in clay
(based on the palm trees in the area) by
the sculptor Llorenç Matamala Pinyol
(1852-1927). The leaf is held in a metal
reticulum, featuring at its intersections
the same floral motif appearing on the
ceramic decoration on the front of the
house.

The **interiors**

The dining room decoration adapts the necessary elements in a unified way and incorporates motifs and representations of nature. The oil paintings on the dining room furniture are by José Torrescassana Sellarés (1845-1918). Particularly interesting are the locks on the furniture, designed by Gaudí and demonstrating his great knowledge of the arts and crafts.

Notice the exuberant decoration between the beams, sculpted in polychrome plaster and in the form of the leaves and fruit of the cherry tree. The wooden beams are supported by Oriental-style corbels on wich carnations are painted.

The chimney is covered with gla ceramic and plaster on the h depicting ivy creeping over the gol background.

Notable is the room known as the *fumoir* —smoking room— on the ground floor, with its own door to the garden. Evocative of Islamic art, this room has wainscoting of yellow and blue glazed tiles on wich are painted carnations, walls tiled with pieces of papiermâché by Hermengildo Miralles and a ceiling of plaster muqarnas (Islamic honeycomb-like decoration) on a brick vault.

The first-floor ceiling —a Baroque-style *trompe l'oeil*— is a pictorial composition featuring, in false perspective, the architectural elements of the house's exterior, combined with leaves of climbing plants and a flock of white doves in a cloudy sky.

THE
GÜELL
ESTATE
PAVILIONS

1884-1887

The Güell Estate is at the top of La Diagonal, in the elegant district of Pedralbes. This area was part of the old municipality of Les Corts de Sarrià, annexed to Barcelona in 1897. With the prolongation of the avenue in the 1920s, the old Güell family estate —given in 1918 for the construction of the Palau Reial, where King Alfons XIII was to lodge— was divided, and is now occupied by the university campus and the Palau de Pedralbes gardens, designed by the architect Nicolau Mª Rubió i Tudurí and opened to the public in 1926.

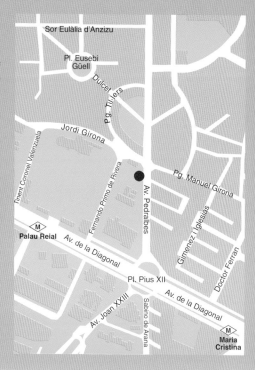

| **Finca Güell** Av. de Pedralbes, 15 | **Metro** Maria Cristina | **Buses** 7, 63, 67, 68, 74, 75, 114 | Open only to researchers. |

Eusebi Güell i Bacigalupi (1846-1918) was an important industrialist, banker and businessman, a typical example of the powerful 19th-century Catalan bourgeoisie. He founded the first companies in Catalonia making Portland cement. He formed part of the governing bodies of important companies such as the Banco Hispano Colonial or the Companyia de Tabacs de Filipines. At the same time, he played a leading role in the flourishing of Catalan culture and was a member of the Lliga Regionalista. Under his patronage Gaudí designed and built his most emblematic works.

The **exteriors** combine masonry, brickwork and ceramic decoration, achieving a rich variety of colours. Gaudí used trencadís —a mosaic of broken pieces— for the first time, an ornamental technique that would characterize all his work.

There is a **single door** made of wrought iron, which hangs on a vertical axis. It was made by the locksmith Joan Oñós.

To the left is the doorkeeper's house, comprising three parts, one octagonal-shaped and two square shaped, crowned by domes.

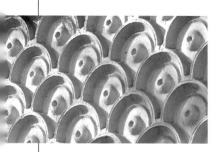

Oriental reminiscences in the *atauriques* (plant-like ornamentation) on the façade.

The group of pavilions made up the gateway to the Güell estate. Gaudí carried out the work between 1884 and 1887.

The ventilation towers and the lantern in the dome suggest the Far Eastern architecture that Gaudí was familiar with from photographs acquired by the School of Architecture.

Latticework, a common feature in Arabic and Oriental countries as a means of ventilation, is adopted by Gaudí with delicate masonry work.

To the right is the old stable with the entrance at one of the corners. It is a rectangular room with transverse parabolic arches that connects with a square pavilion originally designed as an exercise ring for the horses.

Pedestrian gate
Made of wrought iron with dynamic zigzag shapes.

In this phase of his career Gaudí indulges in the combination of historicist themes with structural experimentation. From Oriental art he takes the decoration and from Gothic art the structural plan.

The railings featuring the enchained dragon, one of the most remarkable examples of wrought-iron work in Catalonia, symbolize the eleventh task of Hercules on his voyage to the garden of the Hesperides. The dragon, called Ladon, guarded the garden where the nymphs lived who looked after the golden orange tree, a symbol of love and fertility; Hercules' triumph turned them into splendid trees. The Güell Estate, full of magnificent vegetation, was intended to represent a new garden of the Hesperides.

The dragon, a recurring theme in Gaudí's work, chained, terrifying and dynamic, cannot leave the visitor indifferent. It is not positioned by chance, but the vertices of its head and body allow one to locate the stars forming the Dragon constellation.

The brickwork pillar to the right of the railings is topped off with a piece of sculpture in antimony representing the golden orange tree; in the middle the initial "G", in clear allusion to the owner, Güell, appears surrounded by roses and constitutes a symbolic reference, for these were the prize for the poets taking part in the Jocs Florals poetry competition. Gaudí wished to pay tribute to the Marquis of Comillas, Güell's father-in-law, to whom Cinto Verdaguer dedicated his splendid prize-winning poem *L'Atlàntida* in 1877.

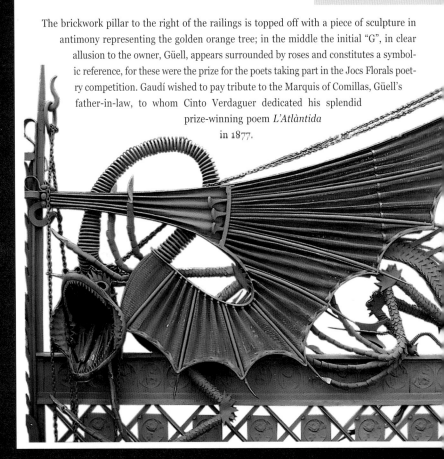

The old **stables** occupy a large rectangular space, with a roof of parabolic arches and brick vaults as architectural elements which give it structure. Between the arches one can see trapezoidal openings allowing an even light into the room. Since 1978 it has been the headquarters of the *Càtedra Gaudí*, directed by the architect Joan Bassegoda; specialized in the architect from Reus, it possesses an important library and a great deal of documentation on the theme of Gaudí.

At the opposite end to the entrance there is a square-shaped room —the old exercise ring— where the stone paving is laid out in concentric circles, placing the Güells' initial in the centre, merely a way of projecting the dome which crowns the pavilion, and which ends in a cupola. It seems as if Gaudí were playing with two basic geometric forms, the sphere and the cube, by placing them one inside the other.

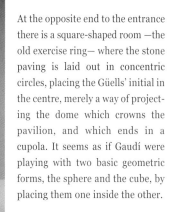

PALAU GÜELL

1886-1888

The Palau Güell is in the Raval district. Originally this was an area of the city which concentrated activities regarded as a nuisance (hospitals, butchers...). Its present boundaries were set in the 14th century by a wall built by King Peter III. In the 19th century, the Raval suffered the impact of the process of industrialisation, with the installation of modern manufacturing processes and, based around the new production model, a new type of workplace grew up: the domestic workshop. In 1886, when Eusebi Güell decided to build his palace, the walls had already been demolished, L'Eixample was beginning to expand and the bourgeoisie were gradually moving out to the new areas well away from the run-down Raval.

 Carrer Nou de la Rambla, 3-5

 Metro Drassanes, Liceu

 Buses 14, 38, 59

 Open: Monday-Saturday, 10am – 2pm and 4pm – 8pm. Closed Sundays and public holidays.

The two **façades**, front and back, have faces of Garraf stone from a quarry owned by the Güell family.

The great long gallery, whose windows give onto the main floor, is the only element which seems to stand out among the apparent simplicity of this façade.

The entrance is indicated by two catenary arches with spectacular wrought-iron railings. These railings are made in such a way that it is possible to observe the street from inside but not to see into the vestibule from the street.

In between the two doors is an original coat of arms of Catalonia in wrought iron, designed by the wrought iron worker Joan Oñós and clearly showing the four bars of the Catalan flag.

The gallery of the back façade comes off the main floor and is crowned by a wrought-iron balcony which is in turn covered by a row of wooden slats to keep the sun off in the manner of a *brise-soleil*. The gallery's decoration is completed by ceramic pieces forming a serpentine silhouette.

In the distribution of the interior space and in the various construction ideas Gaudí showed himself to be far removed from anything done up to that moment and reached a high-point of his career.

The horses entered the **stables** by a ramp emerging from the coach house. The columns, with their mushroom-shaped capitals, and the brick vaults create a spectacular atmosphere. These structural elements —the three central ones are more robust— were done in brick, a simple material considered appropriate for this humble area of the palace.

The main entrance has a double **vestibule** —the interior one is the coach house; in this way the carriages could enter by one door and leave by the other. The floor is of pinewood blocks, which helped to reduce the noise from the stables. The ceiling is formed by extremely flat Byzantine brick vaults. The main staircase is the focal point of the whole area and is flanked by stone columns.

The **hallway** is in the centre of the gallery, which looks on to the main façade. It has five parabolic arcades resting on four columns. On combining with another eight lower ones they are grouped into threes, resting on common triangular plinths.

The **visitors' room** is remarkable for the woodcarving and wrought-iron work on the ceiling and for the curiosity of the latticework, from where the Güell family could observe their visitors without being seen. The sofa in this room is the original one from the palace and dates from the 18th century.

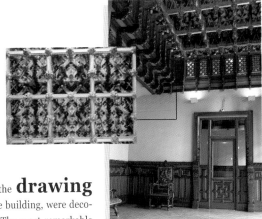

The **dining room** and the **drawing room**, set against the back of the building, were decorated by the architect Camil Oliveras. The most remarkable feature is the extraordinary ceiling formed by wooden coffers combined with pieces of iron arranged spirally, achieving a decorative and structural function, as the floor above has no beams.

The **central salon** is Gaudí's best as from the main floor he creates an empty space, covered by a double cupola —parabolic on the inside and conical on the outside. Square-shaped —measuring 9m by 9m— it is almost 20 m high. The cupola rests on four toral arches and is covered on the inside by hexagonal panels of reddish alabaster. The openings perforating it allow light in and bring to mind the moon and stars.

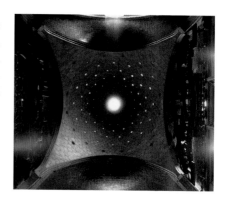

The **viewing gallery**, reached by a staircase, was where the musicians sat. Notice the ebony lattice-work and the marble incrustations.

A small cupboard —a system later used in Casa Batlló— hides a chapel. The room thus had a double use. The interior is covered with panels of gold-plated tinfoil and the doors feature figures of the apostles painted by Aleix Clapés. The rest of the paintings in the room are also by Clapés.

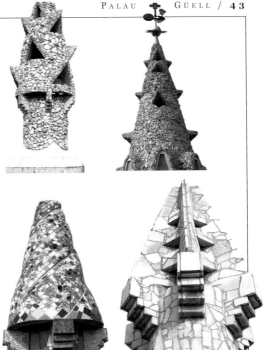

Gaudí gave full vent to his imagination on the roof. The 20 ventilation shafts and chimneys feature different designs: in the centre a cupola shaped like a conical needle rises flanked by four windows in the form of seashells and topped by a bat symbolizing the mediaeval Catalan warriors, a sun, in counterpoint to the moon inside, and the characteristic cross.

The roof terrace is in typical Mediterranean style with long thin bricks, although Gaudí plays with parabolic shapes on the beams which form the roof.

There is a variety of materials: glass, *trencadís*, brick, fragments of vitrified stone and china from the Pickman factory in La Cartuja in Seville.

The College
of the
Teresianes

1888-1889

The Theresians' College is situated in the old municipality of Sant Gervasi, annexed to Barcelona in 1897. This part of the town, at the foot of the Serra de Collserola, quickly became an area of summer residences for the wealthy classes in the second half of the 19th century. At the same time, during this period it also became an important centre for the religious communities devoted to teaching who set up their schools there; we might mention the Mercedarians, the Black Ladies, the order of Saint John and the Theresians, amongst others.

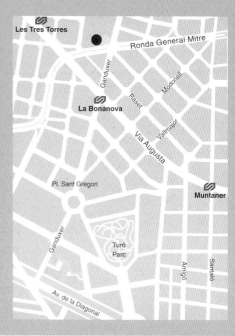

| Carrer de Ganduxer, 85-105 | FGC Bonanova, Tres Torres | Buses 14, 16, 70 74 | Not open to the public |

In 1889 Gaudí was commissioned by Father Enric d'Ossó i Cervelló to continue the work on the Theresians' College, already under way according to a plan by an unknown architect. Ossó had founded the Congregation of Saint Theresa in 1873, made up of nuns devoted to the teaching of the arts, letters and pure and applied sciences to girls, a very novel idea at that time. Some years later they established themselves in Sant Gervasi, the reason why they purchased this land. The college would house the nuns' study centre, the general headquarters of the congregation and a boarding school for girls.

When Gaudí took over the project, the building was already up to the second floor and he quite noticeably altered the plan although he kept the original rectangular layout. In spite of the limited budget, he produced a work of great dignity. It is one his early works —the use of brickwork, the influence of Islamic architecture— where certain elements stand out influenced by Gothic architecture, which would dominate his later work. In appearance it looks like a uniform fortress where only two appendages stick out: the entrance and some servants quarters on the back façade.

The **façade** is characterised by sober decoration with Mudéjar influences; exposed brickwork and stone cover the walls with only patches of ceramic decoration. The composition is based on the repetition of the openings, which differ in size on each floor according to their respective interior purpose, halls on the first two floors and dormitories on the upper floors. The abundant use of parabolic arches on the ground and third floors —much more elaborate— shows the direction his later work was to take.

The **cornice** of the building takes the form of a series of arched battlements amongst which glazed pieces with the letter "T" appear, symbolizing Saint Theresa of Ávila. Until 1936 pieces in the shape of a doctoral biretta, in the saint's honour, were situated on top of the battlements. At the four corners four sharp pinnacles rise, topped with ceramic crosses, which help to emphasize the building's verticality.

Access to the building is through a **portico** formed by a parabolic arch, above which there is a gallery occupying two floors. This projecting part is of exposed brick and masonry. It has narrow windows and brick latticework with clear Mudéjar influences. In the middle appears the Carmelite shield, flanked by two hearts symbolizing the Immaculate Conception and the Transfixion of Saint Theresa. Wrought-iron railings in three parts reproduce the Carmelite symbolism.

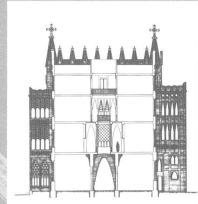

It is in the **interior** where Gaudí achieved his greatest architectural success. The building is organised along a longitudinal axis of communication. On the very high-ceilinged ground floor, the architect designed a corridor above which, on the first floor, a well is situated, introducing some central rectangular patios resembling cloisters, and two long corridors on either side formed by very close parabolic arches so that beams are not necessary to support the floor above. On subsequent floors the ceiling gradually drops and the importance of the corridor is reduced. By creating these successive patios in staggered fashion, Gaudí achieved the penetration of zenithal light and formed dimly lit areas that create an atmosphere of meditation, very appropriate for a convent.

CASA
CALVET

1898 - 1899

Casa Calvet is in the middle of the finest part of L'Eixample, known at the end of the 19th century as the "manufacturers' district". These days warehouses and wholesale cloth and clothes shops occupy its ground floors, a vestige of the important activity which took place in the 18th century in the adjacent district of Sant Pere, traditionally dedicated to the textile industry. This is why the newly-rich middle classes did not move very far from their places of work when the city expanded in 1859.

Gran Via de les Corts Catalanes

Ronda Universitat

Casp

Pl. Urquinaona   Ausiàs Marc

Pl. de Catalunya

 Urquinaona

Fontanella   Ronda Sant Pere

 Catalunya

Av. Portal de l'Àngel

Via Laietana

Carrer de Casp, 48	**Metro** Catalunya, Urquinaona, Gran Via
Buses 7, 16, 17, 22, 24, 28, 39, 45, 48, 50, 54, 56	**Not open to the public**

Casa Calvet was the first terraced house built by Gaudí. He received the commission from the Calvet family, cloth merchants. Very similar in appearance to the other fine buildings typical of this part of L'Eixample, it is a significant landmark in the architect's career, as in it he abandoned mediaeval references and adopted a Modernist approach with certain Baroque overtones. This is the building's most outstanding characteristic, since its composition does not diverge too much from the established norms. Built between 1898 and 1899, Gaudí received the City Council's prize for the best building in the city in 1900.

The **façade**, of Roman-style stone blocks, is of Montjuïc sandstone and is profusely decorated.

Sculptural **central gallery** on the main floor where we can see different types of mushroom depicted, a hobby of the owner's that Gaudí used to create a decorative element.

Trilobular **balcony** with spiral wrought-iron railings.

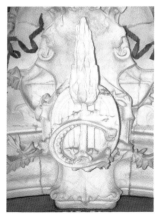

Remarkable for their opulence are the adjacent pillars on the ground floor and the sculptures adorning the main door. We can see the letter "C" for the Calvet surname and the cypress, a symbol of perpetuity

The building comprises a commercial basement and ground floor, a main floor for the Calvet family's use, today occupied by the restaurant Casa Calvet, and four upper floors, with two rented apartments on each.

Undulating cornice with the busts of the three patron saints of Vilassar de Mar, the owner's birthplace.

In the **entrances** mention should be made of the architect's meticulousness, seeking always to embellish with a certain leaning towards the Baroque.

Doorbells

Door handle on the main door.

The house number.

The lift door is framed by two sets of helicoidal Solomonic columns in artificial granite.

The lift cabin is an excellent piece of work where wood, iron and glass alternate harmoniously.

On the walls and joins of the arches on the staircase one can see the inscription *"Fe, Patria, Amor"* (Faith, Homeland, Love) in allusion to the Jocs Florals poetry competition.

Among the **furniture** designed for the Casa Calvet, the perfect combination of form and function in designs which still seem contemporary today catches the eye.

Chairs and sofa, part of the office furniture (now on display in the Museu Casa Gaudí). In carved oak and with organic shapes, they were made by the Barcelona firm of Casas & Bardés.

The most spectacular proposal can be seen on the **back façade**, which Gaudí gave a special pre-eminence by alternating balconies and columned galleries, producing chiaroscuro lighting effects and letting in the maximum amount of sunlight.

The back façade, in artificial stone and plastered brickwork, is much more personal than the front.

The patio on the main floor, adorned with artificial stone jardinières, embellishes the interior of the entire block.

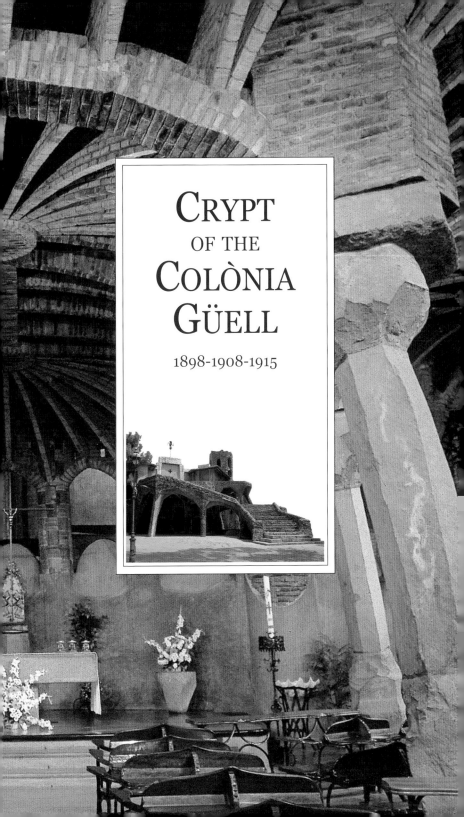

CRYPT
OF THE
COLÒNIA
GÜELL

1898-1908-1915

The Colònia Güell in Santa Coloma de Cervelló is the most important of the industrial villages on the River Llobregat, created in the 19th century. Owned by Eusebi Güell and Ferran Alsina, cloth makers, it was established in 1890. It features two distinct parts: the residential area and the factory, composed of different industrial buildings and a tall chimney. Houses for the factory workers were built, as well as basic services: a library, a store and the church, designed by Gaudí. Architects such as Francesc Berenguer and Joan Rubió i Bellver collaborated with Gaudí in the construction of the buildings. The factory closed for good in 1973.

On the road from Sant Boi to Sant Vicenç dels Horts

Ferrocarrils de la Generalitat: Molí Nou (Martorell line)

Buses from Barcelona
L70 (Plaça Espanya to Sant Boi) and L76 (Sant Boi to the village)

Open to the public

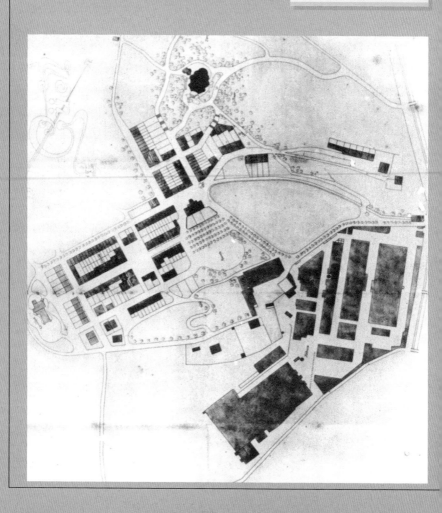

Gaudí was commissioned to build a church for the village in 1898. The foundation stone was laid in October 1908 and building work continued until 1915, when the project was halted. Only the crypt was actually built. During this period Gaudí made many studies to obtain new structural solutions. The crypt of the Güell industrial village was actually a testing ground, the results of which he was later to apply to the Sagrada Família.

Sketch by Gaudí of the outside of the church, which reminds one of the Sagrada Família.

By means of this inverted model, Gaudí tried out his structural proposals which were to lead him to surpass the principles of Gothic architecture. The model allowed him to do without mathematical calculations. It was made of strings representing the columns and arches; from them he hanged small bags filled with shotgun pellets in proportion to the weight to be calculated. The model was photographed and the final form obtained by reversing the image.

The **portico** of sloping columns and irregular shapes is the antechamber to the crypt and seems to be a continuation of the natural pinewood surroundings.

The vaults were built for the first time as hyperbolic paraboloids, according to traditional Catalan vaulting.

Detail of the vaults.

The mosaic on the top part of the door shows in the centre the insignia of the Virgin Mary. It is flanked by the four cardinal virtues: Justice in the form of a pair of scales, Strength with a knight's suit of armour and helmet, for Prudence he uses a moneybox, whilst the knife cutting bread and a *porró* (drinking vessel) symbolize Temperance. Above we can see the burning cross and the symbols for Alpha and Omega.

The windows are of different sizes according to the need dictated by the structure. The windows are decorated with the symbols for Alpha and Omega and a *trencadís* cross.

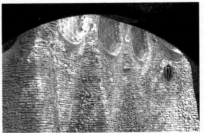

The railings are made of scrap material derived from the unusable needles from the textile machinery. J.M. Jujol's participation seems clear in the manufacture of these decorative materials.

The perimeter **walls** have an undulating shape. This irregularity is heightened by the use of brick and black basaltic stone which give it an intended rough appearance.

The practically **flat ceiling** produces a great variety of structural forms. Irregularity is the dominant theme. On occasions the brick ribbing branches out, on others the joins between the columns and vaults are made in staggered form. It is a marvellous lesson in architecture.

Ambulatory. The central columns support the ceiling ribbing.

Outstanding are the four sloping **columns** of basaltic stone. Despite their stark appearance they do not fail to include capital, shaft and base.

Gaudí especially sought the entry of natural light in his buildings. Through the windows and stained glass, although the originals disappeared in 1936, he achieved a surprising amount of illumination even though it was a crypt.

Detail of the brick ribbing running along the vaults

Continuous concrete **pav-ing** dating from the time of construction.

The benches were originally designed by Gaudí and are made from wood and iron.

BELLESGUARD

1900-1909

The Bellesguard Tower is in the upper part of the district of Sant Gervasi de Cassoles in the area bordering on the Serra de Collserola. Until the mid-19th century, Sant Gervasi was a town with a low population density and scattered dwellings, except in the part around the church which lent its name to the place in the early Middle Ages. Cosy and healthy, this atmosphere attracted the aristocracy and middle classes of Barcelona, who traditionally set up their summer residences there. In 1897 Sant Gervasi became part of the municipality of Barcelona.

| 🚶 Carrer del Bellesguard, 16-20 | 🚌 Buses 22, 58, 64, 73, 75 | ✖ Not open to the public Access to the garden only |

A. T. V. — 71 - BARCELONA
Camino de Bellesguard

Bellesguard was an old royal residence built in 1408 by King Martin I the Humane. It was possibly his secretary, Bernat Metge, who gave the name meaning "with a pleasant view" to the house, due to its privileged position. The king was married there to Margarita de Prades by Pope Benedict XIII in 1409.

The stone viaduct resting on sloping columns is a clear precursor of the much more elaborate forms seen in the Park Güell. Gaudí built this retaining wall to divert the path through the grounds to the Sant Gervasi cemetery.

The overall appearance of the house, commissioned in 1900 by Maria Sagués, widow of Sr. Figueras, recalls Gothic building and reminds one of a defensive tower. Gaudí conceived an austere, sober enclosed space with few windows, almost all in Neo-Gothic style. The practically square floor plan —with a small semi-hexagonal part and a slender tower attached— helps to reinforce this impression.

The use of local materials —slate in green and grey shades— allowed Gaudí to blend the building into the surroundings. The way he obtained the slabs from prefabricated pieces is interesting. Gaudí placed small stones on a plaster mould base and then spread the mortar over them. He was to use this system later in the Park Güell.

Small walkway around the roof which Le Corbusier later adopted in his buildings ("promenades architectoniques") and which also constitutes a mediaeval reference.

Above the staircase, situated at the western corner, a high tower rises topped with an arrow ending in a Catalan flag with spiral bars, the royal crown and the cross, so habitual in Gaudí's architecture, pointing towards the cardinal points of the compass.

The triforal windows, the semicircular arch over the entrance and the battlements are a very personal recreation by Gaudí of Catalan civil Gothic.

In the **interior**, the architect managed to introduce a style completely unrelated to the exterior Gothicism. He proposed different ways of covering the ceilings, tried out peculiar combinations of light and shapes and in general experimented with the most diverse structural systems. All the walls and ceilings, except for the two   attics, are covered in white plaster.

The house's dining room ceiling features very slender plastered brick projecting arches. With this structure, beams are not necessary.

The first attic has a continuous loggia of windows, which take the form of battlements on the outside. Its structure is formed from eight pillars rising from the floor below. The pillars have capitals made in projecting brick and support a flat brick slab. From here a series of arches in the form of an irregular fan spread out to the perimeter walls.

On top of the first attic, and in line with the idea of giving buildings two-level roofing as in Casa Batlló, there is a second attic. It is a room with an ogival brick vault and trilobular arched windows. On top there is a small terrace.

PARC
GÜELL

1901-1914

The Park Güell occupies a pre-eminent part of the city on the southern slopes of the Muntanya Pelada (Bare Mountain), a small rocky outcrop to the north of the plain of Barcelona, culminating in the El Carmel and La Rovira hills. The dwellings in this essentially rural environment were typically ancestral houses possessing large areas of land. The good view and healthy atmosphere were the reasons why this area filled up with villas belonging to rich families in the second half of the 19th century, giving rise to the district of La Salut (Health), which probably got its name from being close to a chapel dedicated to the Virgin of La Salut.

| Carrer d'Olot, s/n | **Metro** Vallcarca, Lesseps | **Buses** 24, 25, 28, 31, 32, 74 | **Open to the public** |

In 1899, the financier Eusebi Güell bought the Can Muntaner de Dalt estate with the idea of creating a garden city in the English style and, in line with the town planning tendencies of the moment, getting close to nature. A year later, Gaudí was commissioned to study this initiative, which apparently must have interested the bourgeoisie who were developing the new residential area in an expanding city. A second estate purchased in 1902 from Ramon Coll i Pujol increased the amount of land available for the project.

As the area is situated at a height of between 150 and 210 metres above sea level on steep uneven ground, the architect decided on a landscape design and architectural style respectful of the surrounding environment and vegetation. In spite of this, the housing development was a failure, and only two of the sixty planned houses were actually built. One of them is now the Casa Gaudí Museu, where the architect lived for almost 20 years. After the land had been acquired by Barcelona City Council, it was made into a public park in 1922. In 1969 it was declared of artistic interest and in 1984, world heritage by UNESCO.

The Park Güell, built between 1901 and 1914, occupies some 15 hectares of land and constitutes one of the most ambitious works undertaken by Gaudí.

The triangular-shaped plots were laid out according to the idea that the houses, once built, should have a good view of Barcelona and be conveniently sunny. More than 50% of the total surface area was preserved as green space.

From carrer d'Olot, one enters the park through a main gate flanked by two strange-looking **pavilions** —destined to be the doorkeeper's house and the administration office— both oval with dome-shaped roofs and covered in polychrome mosaic. Attached to the outer wall, they guard the area as if they were two crenellated towers on a mediaeval castle.

The **perimeter wall** is seen at its finest in Carrer d'Olot. It is of local stone masonry and the top is a bell-shaped cornice covered in red and white *trencadís*. Some round medallions, integrated in the line of the cornice like cigar bands, announce the "Park Güell". This same wall, free of decorative elements, encloses the entire area of the park, highlighting Eusebi Güell's idea of creating a select and well-looked-after residential district.

The door decorated with palmetto leaves on the main gate, replacing the original wooden one, was set in place in 1965, having been removed from Casa Vicens.

The pavilion on the right-hand side was the doorkeeper's house. It has two parts – one long with round ends, facing the street, and another one behind, where we find the entrance through a porch supported by a stone column. On the ground floor there are four chambers: vestibule, dining room, kitchen and doorkeeper's office. The toilets are on the landing, and on the first floor there are four bedrooms. The attic covered with hyperboloidal brick vaults has two side terraces with battlements. It was possible to reach a viewpoint situated around the ventilation tower by a spiral staircase.

The window frames, cornices and battlements are made from prefabricated pieces of long thin brick covered with *trencadís*.

This tower, almost 30 metres high, is hyperboloidal in section and hollow inside. Its external surfaces are undulating and covered in a blue and white chessboard pattern, and topped by a metal piece shaped like a chalice that supports the pedestal and cross. The arms of this cross, as in the Bellesguard house, point towards the four cardinal points of the compass. It was restored by Adolf Florensa in 1952.

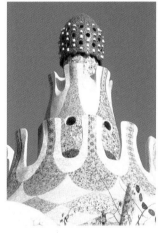

The highly imaginative interior of the pavilion on the left-hand side comprises a square room, two apsidal chambers with parabolic arches and a fourth from which one gains access by a curved staircase to the second floor, equipped with side terraces. The stairway leading inside the tower comes off one of them.

The rooftops are made of undulating surfaces crowned by a ventilation tower shaped like an *Amanita Muscaria* mushroom. The mushroom-shaped element was used by Gaudí in Casa Calvet.

Grotto situated to the right of the double staircase designed for four horse-drawn carriages, with a parabolic vault supported by a hollow central column. Using a large slice of imagination, it looks to some extent like an elephant.

Stairs leading to the Hypostyle Forum, flanked by undulating walls decorated with pieces of multicoloured *trencadís* alternating with white ones in draughtboard fashion. In the centre there is a series of basins where the water flows, with surprising jets evoking zoomorphic figures full of symbolism and mythological allusions.

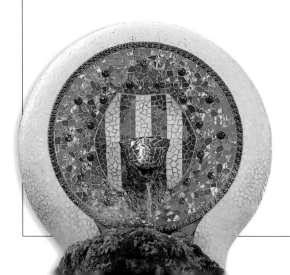

Medallion with a toric frame decorated with predominantly blue and white *trencadís*.

A snake-like animal's head emerges from the convex part, where we can see a Catalan flag.

This great tank designed by Gaudí in brick pillars and very low vaults and water-proofed in a very novel fashion with Portland cement, collected the rainwater which filtered from the Plaça del Teatre Grec, through pipes ingeniously situated in the axes of the Doric columns.

The water collected, up to 12,000 cubic metres, was for the housing estate's exclusive use.

One of the most emblematic figures in the park is the ceramic dragon (or lizard or salamander), where the water flows out from the underground cistern below the Hypostyle Forum. It stands in the centre of the flight of steps at the foot of the colonnaded gallery, a majestic guardian of the waters hidden below ground, as did the snake Python after being defeated and entombed by Apollo in the omphalos of the temple of Delphi.

Josep M. Jujol i Gibert (born Tarragona 1879 – died Barcelona 1949). A versatile architect and creator with a boundless imagination. The use of everyday objects in his ornamentation made him the precursor of the artistic avant-garde and his surprising artistic creations are close to surrealism. His work included both architecture and the design of furniture and other domestic fittings. Outstanding examples of his work are the Teatre Metropol in Tarragona, the Torre de la Creu and the Casa Negre in Sant Joan Despí, Casa Planells in Barcelona and the church at Vistabella, among others.

Continuing with his historicist tendencies Gaudí designed the **Sala Hipòstila** (Hypostyle Forum), destined to be the garden city's marketplace, like a great Doric temple. This colonnaded space also acts as a structural support for the Plaça del Teatre Grec, at the top of the flight of steps.

It is made up of 86 columns set in ordered symmetry, the central ones standing vertically and the perimeter ones slightly inclined in order to increase the force of containment. They are all identical, with a grooved shaft and a capital with an octagonal abacus. Sculpted from masonry, they are covered with white *trencadís* on the lower half. Gaudí left out five columns, possibly to create more spacious areas, and in their place put multicoloured *trencadís* panels evoking the four seasons on the ceiling, the work of his close collaborator Josep Mª. Jujol.

Sitting on top of the columns are prefabricated domes with a spherical cap covered in white *trencadís*, with vividly coloured ceiling roses with motifs alluding to the lunar cycle in their centre.

The site is topped by a terraced cornice featuring a sinuous surface of ornamental *trencadís* forming the back of the bench encircling the upper *piazza*. Gargoyles in the form of lions' heads are placed in the concave areas of the frieze, and borders of four drops of rain about to fall evoke the rainwater as it trickles and drips.

La Plaça del Teatre Grec is situated in a natural bowl, partly built on firm ground, and partly on the artificial structure supported by the columns of the Hypostyle Forum. Measuring over 3,000 square metres, it was designed to be the agora of the garden city. From here there is a lovely view of Barcelona and the Mediterranean which so inspired Gaudí.

Along the hillside runs a circular path affording good view. Facing the sea, the protruding square is encircled by the original serpentine **bench** which also serves as a barrier. Both are splendid places to walk and sit, and take in the natural surrounding

Josep Mª Jujol used the *collage* technique for the ceramic decoration of the bench, incrusting a great variety of materials on a mud base: plates, bottles, glasses, cups etc. In this way, he achieved extraordinary geometric, floral and zoomorphic designs. In a second phase, Jujol applied colour to these fragments of *trencadís* which, submitted to repeated firing and protected with vitrifiable varnish, acquired resistance to erosion. They are now valued as an excellent artistic creation.

Marian inscriptions written in Latin and Catalan.

Gaudí designed easy-to-assemble prefabricated pieces for the construction of this bench. His concept was based on anatomical considerations —note the supporting ridge for the lumbar regions of the back— and its appearance doubtlessly sprang from the architect's imagination and ingenuity.

The creation of a network of easily accessible pathways, adapted to the lie of the land and in harmony with the surroundings, is another of Park Güell's triumphs. Three kilometres of

paths, ramps, viaducts and bridges

allow access to all areas, achieving their complete integration in the landscape and avoiding the classic resort to terracing. For this, Gaudí erected structures comprising prefabricated elements —pillars, columns, capitals, arches and brick vaults— which he then covered with rustic stone from the area. By using truncated cones and helixes, he achieved easily recognisable decorative motifs taken from nature.

There are some main roads, achieved with extreme originality, differentiated in form according to the lie of the land and the necessary equilibrium of the forces of containment: The **main road** is a wide path bordered with natural and artificial palm trees which leads to the rest of the paths. A series of stone spheres along the path symbolizes the Christian rosary and reminds us of the importance of religion in the architectural language of Gaudí's work

Font de Sant Salvador

Casa de Martí
Trias i Domènech

Pont de

La Bugadera   Via
Principal   Pont del
Mig

Sala Hipòstila   Museu
Can Muntaner   Gau

Plaça del
Teatre Grec   Pont de Baix

Turó de
les Menes

The portico that passes behind Eusebi Güell's house (formerly Casa Larrard, now a state school) is known in its first stretch as the *Pòrtic de la Bugadera* (the Washerwoman's Portico) —we can see the figure of a woman with the washing basket on her head, and who originally held a washing pole in her hand. An interesting structure is that generated to support the thrust of the natural slope, made up of inclined columns and very elongated vaults that at the same time act as a pathway. Notice the semicircular ramp with spiral columns at the end of the portico.

The Pont de Baix (Lower Bridge) at the bottom of the main road, leads to the Casa-Museu Gaudí and is made of two lines of sloping columns evoking palm trees. The leaves joined together form the vaults. The raised part of the viaduct contains rustic benches arranged irregularly and flowerpot holders planted with agaves.

The upper viaduct, known as the Pont de Dalt (Upper Bridge) is composed of three lines of columns with ribbed vaults and *plementería* formed by the uniform arrangement of stones. Set against the sloping columns there are some benches with a back that invite the walker to rest awhile. Notice the mushroom-shaped flowerpot holders that border the top of the path alternating with rustic stone benches and delicate railings that resemble lace work.

The viaduct called the Pont del Mig (Middle Bridge) starts near the gate leading to Carretera del Carmel. It is made up of three lines of columns —vertical in the centre and sloping on the outside. The vaults, of semicircular arches covered with small stones, are arranged in parallel and contrast with the large stones set like stalactites as *plementería* (filling) of the arches.

During the excavation and levelling work on the land destined for the **Park Güell**, a prehistoric cave from the quaternary era was discovered, with fossil and bone remains, at the foot of a hill in the southwest corner of the area. This place, known as the Turó de les Menes (Mines Hill), overlooked the housing development and was chosen by Gaudí for the construction of a chapel which was to have resembled the crypt at the Güell Industrial Village. This idea never got any further than the raising of a piece of rustic stone, like a megalithic monument.

Polygonal in shape, this tower-viewpoint has a crucifixion scene on top with three crosses overlooking the city, and can be reached by steps. These crosses were destroyed in 1936 and restored in 1939, though not strictly according to Gaudí's original design.

The Muntanya Pelada, (Bare Mountain) as its name well indicates, was originally an area of sparse vegetation. Gaudí proposed the green zone of the housing estate as a natural space where herbaceous plants and trees could grow freely. Mediterranean vegetation was ideally the most suitable to adapt to the climate and grow without problems. Carob trees, oaks, pines and evergreen oaks were added to the already existing bushes, and in time would form the splendid woods today easily crossed by earthen paths and narrow steps that allow the visitor to enter the more thickly-wooded areas.

Saint Salvador's Fountain, remodelled in 1984 by J.M. Casamor.

This house was built by Francesc Berenguer Mestres and was designed originally as a model for the houses in the garden city. Gaudí acquired it in 1906 and lived there until the time he moved to the Sagrada Família. In 1963 the house was purchased by the association "Amics de Gaudí" (Friends of Gaudí) and turned into a museum where, basically, furniture designed by the architect is displayed.

Can Muntaner, an original house on the estate, where Eusebi Güell spent the last years of his life. In 1923 it was turned into a state school.

Martí Trias i Domènech's house, built by Juli Batllerell i Arús. It occupies two plots of land purchased at the start of the garden city development, and is still occupied today by members of the same family.

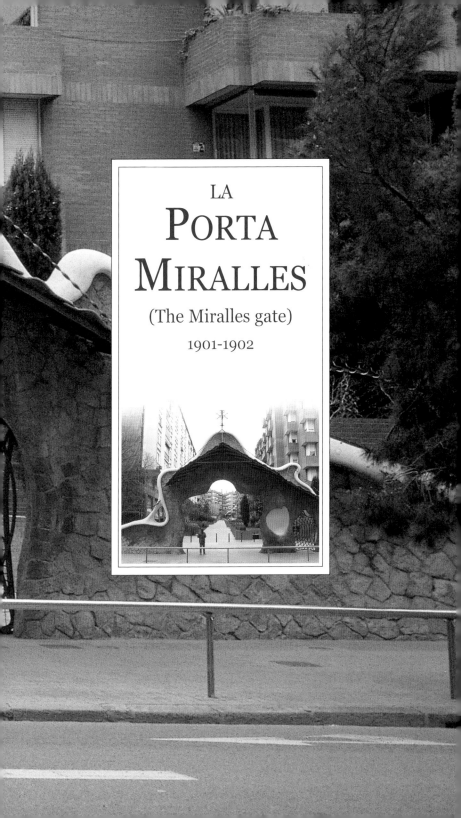

LA
PORTA
MIRALLES

(The Miralles gate)

1901-1902

The gate to the Miralles estate is in the district of Sarrià, an old town annexed to Barcelona in 1921. This is one of the few significant pieces together with the Güell estate, not very far away, vestiges of the great summer residential estates belonging to the important Barcelona families in this area at the beginning of the 20th century. Today the urban landscape has changed radically and although development has been intense, it is still a quality building. The Miralles gate partly encloses a group of buildings designed in 1968 by the architect José Antonio Coderch de Sentmenat, known as "Les Cotxeres" (The Tramsheds) because the Barcelona trams were kept there during their lifetime.

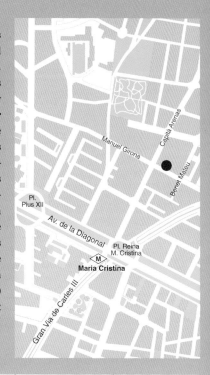

| Carrer de Manuel Girona, 55-61 | **Metro** Maria Cristina | **Buses** 6, 7, 16, 33, 74 | **Open to the public** |

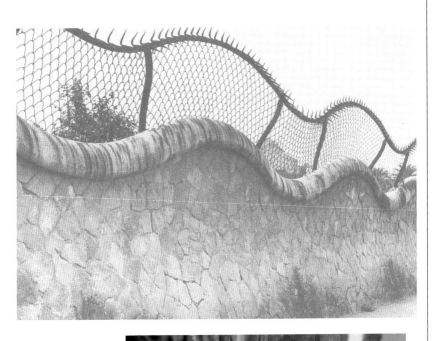

In 1901 Gaudí was commissioned by Hermengildo Miralles, a well-known printer of the day, to design an entrance gate and perimeter wall for his estate, located on what was then a private road belonging to the Güell family, today Carrer de Manuel Girona. Miralles was known as a publisher and also as the manufacturer of pieces of papier-mâché imitating glazed wall tiles and which, in the building trade, were intended to replace the traditional ceramic covering.

Only part of the **wall** and **gate**, although altered, remains of the perimeter designed by Gaudí in 1901-1902. It is characterised by marked undulating lines. It has two doors, the main one, wider —originally for carriages— in the form of a lobular arch, as well as a side door that served as an entrance for pedestrians, and conserves the original iron bars. Both are protected by a canopy covered with tiles featuring zoomorphic shapes.

The **wall**, built in rough masonry, is topped by spiked metallic railings. This design of railing is very similar to that used in 1904 at the back of Casa Batlló.

The **cross** is an element widely used by Gaudí. It was set in place in 1902, disappeared at a later date, and was replaced in its original position after the restoration work in 1978. It is a four-armed cross with a sinuous shape made of wrought iron. There is a replica in the Gaudí Museum and another in the church of the Güell industrial village.

The tortoise —shell— shape **tiles** show us the importance of symbolism based on the animal kingdom used by Gaudí in his work. Originally made in pieces of papier-mâché, today they are of fibrous cement.

On the wall separating the two doors there is a **recess** where the estate owner's name must have been set originally, made from papier-mâché tiles.

Sculpture of Gaudí by Quim Camps, installed in 1999, when the latest restoration work was carried out at the site.

Casa
Batlló

1904-1906

C asa Batlló is in the heart of L'Eixample in Passeig de Gràcia, a tree-lined avenue that was opened in 1827 as a main thoronghfare in the new city and which, after 1859, would attract the wealthy Barcelona bourgeoisie. In the early 20th century beautiful houses proliferated, rich in ornamental decoration, adapted to the hygiene standards of the time and designed by renowned local architects. If we observe the buildings near to Casa Batlló, we shall see two more splendid examples of Catalan Modernism making up what has become known as the "Mançana de la Discòrdia" (The Block of Discord): Casa Amatller, by Josep Puig i Cadafalch and Casa Lleó Morera, by Lluís Domènech i Montaner, on the corner of Carrer Consell de Cent.

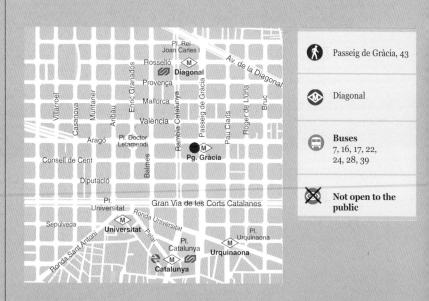

Passeig de Gràcia, 43

Diagonal

Buses
7, 16, 17, 22, 24, 28, 39

Not open to the public

Casa Batlló resulted from the commission given by Josep Batlló to Antoni Gaudí to reform an already existing building completed in 1877. Work was carried out between 1904 and 1906 with the help of important professionals.

The radical transformation effected converted an anodyne house into a prodigious construction where light and colour confer dream-like contrasts. In this building Gaudí, leaving behind his previous historicist references and advancing in the search for very personal structural and ornamental solutions, created the culminating example of Catalan Modernism.

Gaudí carried out a complete restoration: he modified the inner courtyard, dismantled the ground and first floors, created a new back façade, crowned the front of the house with a two-storey attic hidden behind an undulating roof and gave a new look to the back courtyard.

Although the building was originally meant only for apartments —the main one occupied by the owner and the rest rented out following the usual practice in L'Eixample— today it houses offices as well, and on the main and ground floors various reception rooms, following the alterations carried out in the 1990s by the present owners.

Gaudí was well aware that the house was next to Casa Amatller, built by the architect Josep Puig i Cadafalch in 1900. He moved the tower, originally intended for the centre, to one side, designed a small terrace to avoid the party wall being seen and created a moulding between the houses.

The **façade** wall was made thinner to form slight undulations; there he placed round pieces of ceramic and fragments of glass in blue-green shades which remind one of a sea bed and evoke Monet's series of water lilies. Gaudí personally directed the setting of the pieces from the street, indicating to the workmen, supplied with baskets of coloured glass pieces, where they should place them. Some experts are of the opinion that he was assisted in this by Josep Mª. Jujol. The façade is a magnificent sight in the early morning, and looks spectacular at night when it is lit up.

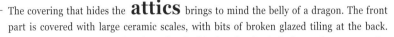

The covering that hides the **attics** brings to mind the belly of a dragon. The front part is covered with large ceramic scales, with bits of broken glazed tiling at the back. Multicoloured cylindrical and spherical pieces alternate on the monster's supposed backbone. At the side, like a lance, a tower rises, ending in what seems to be a flower bulb and finished off with a cross, recreating the legend of Saint George, the patron saint of Catalonia. There are still more symbolic elements, like the three monograms of Jesus (JHS), Joseph (JHP) and Mary (M), and the arms of the cross pointing to the cardinal points of the compass.

The enigmatic stone **balconies** with iron railings create sinuous shapes and have attracted many interpretations. The most common is that of masks which, together with the roof resembling a Harlequin's cap, might suggest an allegory of the Carnival. Others, however, think they see sad-eyed skulls. Nevertheless, despite his overflowing imagination, it seems unlikely that Gaudí had such ideas in mind.

Gaudí radically redesigned the **gaps in the façade** on these floors. He created enormous openings made by a series of windows in Montjuïc stone separated by very slim columns that bring to mind bones. These hyperboloidal elements were a foretaste of what was to come in La Pedrera. The windows in the main floor gallery were an exceptional novelty, as with no wooden frames in the windows it is possible to open them completely and get a panoramic view of Passeig de Gràcia.

To make the most of the light entering, the **inner courtyard** was covered with ceramic pieces, flat and in relief, designed by Gaudí himself. The colour changes gradually from cobalt blue, on the upper floors, to white, passing through sky blue and pearl grey. The windows get bigger as one descends in order to increase the illumination. The patio is crowned by skylight made from iron parabolic shapes.

The **entrance to the building** is almost intricate, seemingly to allow us to gaze with amazement on the magnificent interior: the bottom of the wooden staircase to the main floor, the lift, the plaster ceilings, the courtyard, or details such as bars or doorbells. Unfortunately the wooden wainscoting disappeared in the 1940s.

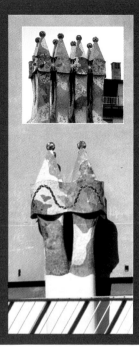

On the **rooftop** are groups of chimneys with spiral stacks – reminding us of natural elements such as flames or whirlwinds. The tubes are clad with glass panels and appear crowned by conical prisms topped off by spheres, also of glass. At the join between the tube and the prism we can see ceramic flowers.

The roof was originally paved with geometrically shaped coloured tiles.

In Casa Batlló there are two **attics** on top with parabolic brick vaults, which we will see again in much more spectacular fashion in Casa Milà. Gaudí believed that houses should have a double roof just as the important people in his day and age wore a hat and carried a parasol. It is structurally justified because in this way it creates a part of the house distinct from the rest of the building, taking on more elasticity, and also allows the building to better withstand the ravages of time.

Gaudí's oak **furniture** is strong and durable; its chief characteristic lies in its carving. Curved lines predominate in the forms and volumes, both in the furniture and in the ornamental elements in general, creating unique homogenous atmospheres.

Observation of the photograph of the dining room on the main floor, the former Batlló family residence, allows us to see the extraordinary wealth of the original design. Unfortunately, many elements have disappeared, like the chapel situated in the main living room which could be hidden behind sliding doors, and which contained a beautiful relief of the Holy Family by Josep Llimona. The magnificent ceilings that formed eddies and all kinds of surprising shapes have also disappeared, eliminated in 1961. Fortunately, some of the pieces of furniture are kept in the Museu Gaudí, in Parc Güell.

The double chairs —two chairs joined together in the same piece— were conceived so that one could sit together with someone else. Their concave backs mould perfectly to the shape of the body.

Gaudí's knowledge of the craftsman's art, which he had learned in childhood, gave him a significant advantage over his far more theoretical fellow architects, and gave his architecture a special seal. His buildings are full of all kinds of craftsmanship. This is the reason for him wishing to extend his ideas to the everyday objects that he designed and even built with his own hands.

The chairs belong to the same series but are smaller and their backs are simpler. Their legs are cylindrical and slightly twisted.

The inspiration from nature can be f⬤ the anatomical design of the chairs re⬤ bling the shapes of bones and the valv⬤ molluscs. Popular themes are to be se⬤ the beautiful chimney on the main ⬤ bringing to mind the high-backed ber⬤ in Catalan country houses.

The **back façade** is far simpler but has a great personality. It uses snake-like forms on the top and decoration in the form of garlands made with fragments of glazed tiles that we can also see on the balcony tiles and on the edges of the façade. The terrace railings are made up of several pieces joined together which reproduce a net design, a motif that Gaudí was to use again on other projects.

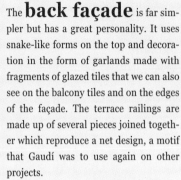

Gaudí did not overlook a single detail in the design of the building, and for this reason on the rail enclosing the **back courtyard** he reproduced ornamentation that confers unity on the whole project; this is the case of the central element of the rail around the courtyard, decorated with the same ceramic pieces as the façade.

CASA
MILÀ

1906 - 1912

The Casa Milà is on the corner of Carrer Provença and Passeig de Gràcia, on the edge of the town of Gràcia when it was incorporated into Barcelona in 1897. El Camí de Jesús —now Passeig de Gràcia— was the shortest route from El Portal de l'Àngel to Gràcia. Fountains and gardens sprang up along this avenue —the so-called Camps Elisis— and it was a place of recreation for the people of Barcelona. As it had become an important thoroughfare, the Barcelona bourgeoisie built their most significant houses there. Today this atmosphere can still be felt on one of the most elegant avenues in Europe.

| Passeig de Gràcia, 92 | **Metro** Diagonal | **Buses** 7, 16, 17, 22, 24, 28, 39 |  **Opening times**. Espai Gaudí and the Apartment in La Pedrera: daily from 10 am to 8 pm |

9
SMITh

LA CÀSA DEN GAUDÍ
—Mamà ¿que també hi ha hagut terratrèmols aquí?

The **Casa Milà**, in allusion to the building's developers, Pere Milà and Roser Segimon, who commissioned Gaudí to build it in 1906, is popularly known as La Pedrera (The Quarry), due to the huge quantity of stone blocks used in its facade. It is the fourth and last example of Gaudí's work in Passeig de Gràcia. The first two —which have since disappeared— were the Gilbert pharmacy (1879) and the decoration in the Bar Torino (1902), the third was the Casa Batlló (1904-1906), followed by the Casa Milà.

La Pedrera gave rise to a lively controversy during its construction due to its surprising shape. Proof of this are the satyrical comments and jokes which appeared in various publications.

Sculpture or Architecture?

The **façade** is made up of large blocks of stone. It seems to be a single unit because Gaudí had the edges of the stones cut in order to create uniformity. The facade has no load-bearing function but serves as a curtain wall. The blocks are joined to the wrought-iron work using pieces of metal emerging from the girders. This solution allowed him to create large openings.

Gaudí managed to create a dream-like façade in which abstraction, expressionism and surrealism are fused.

Gaudí's religiousness can be clearly seen from these inscriptions: Ave, Gratia, Plena, Dominus, Tecum, in reference to the Virgin Mary. The writing is characteristic of his colleague Jujol.

Calcareous stone from Vilafranca del Penedès, less durable than that used on the ground floor. Gaudí opted for austere colours in contrast to his immediately previous work, Casa Batlló.

Highly durable stone from the quarries of El Garraf.

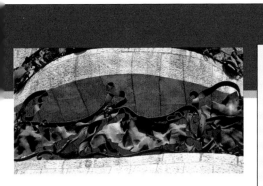

The **railings**, all different although presenting a clear unity, were made from recycled iron. Josep Mª. Jujol is thought to have played an important part in their fabrication. This iron work might be interpreted in a dream-like way as seaweed washed up on imaginary cliffs.

La Pedrera has given rise to numerous interpretations. For some, its undulation symbolises the movement of the sea.

Others see a direct reference to mountain chains like the Serra de Prades, close to his birthplace, Sant Miquel del Fai or the cliffs at Pareis in Majorca. Perhaps it is Mother Nature, generally speaking the constant source of inspiration in all his work.

Gaudí entrusted a great work of sculpture to Carles Maní, featuring the Virgin of the Rosary – in the owner's honour – flanked by the archangels Saint Michael and Saint Gabriel, which was to crown the facade. This in fact was never put in place; perhaps Gaudí thought it might spoil the building's harmony and proportions.

The old coal cellars were eliminated in 1932 and turned into shops. Initially they featured specially designed iron bars similar to the railings at the back of the house. Today only two small examples remain.

The two circular **courtyards** act as facades. Gaudí was very careful with the details: paintings, railings...These two elements become the driving force of the entire building, in this way clearly superior to the traditional courtyards of the corner buildings in Cerdà's Eixample, situated in line with the central doorway. Access to the main floor from the courtyard of the entrance in Passeig de Gràcia is by means of a covered staircase. The short climb is embellished by many decorative details: exquisite colour schemes, the wrought-iron railings interspersed with flowerpot-holders, or the columns

of rough-hewn stone joined to the ceiling in many different ways. The rest of the staircases are in secondary courtyards.

The wrought-iron door with its transparency facilitates the flow of communication between the street and the interior.

The **paintings** offer a colourful counterpoint to the building's chromatic austerity. They were done in oils on plaster.

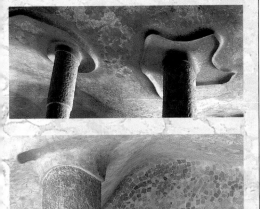

Highly colourful decorative paintings in the courtyards.

Paintings on a floral theme imitating the *trencadís* technique.

Academic-style mural paintings by Aleix Clapés inspired by 16th century tapestries on mythological themes hanging in the Royal Palace in Madrid.

The **interiors** allow us to imagine middle-class family life in the early-20th century.

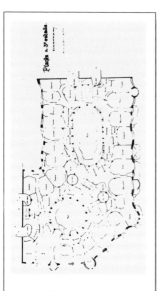

In one of his early drafts, Gaudí did away completely with straight lines and placed the stairs in the main courtyards.

A model of the floor tile designed and made by Ga in person. Taking its inspi tion, as usual, from nature featured the shapes of octopus, a star and a snail. Produced by the Escc company, Passeig de Grà has been paved with th since the 1960s following initiative by Barcelona C Council.

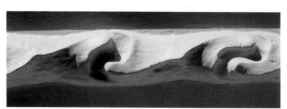

The photographs at the top of the page are of the apartment restored in 1998 by the Fundació Caixa de Catalunya. Apart from the undeniable value of visiting a typical flat in the building (actually, two have been joined together), it allows us to get a taste of the period in which it was occupied (from 1911 on).

Between 1954 and 1955, the architect F.J. Barba Corsini made a series of alterations to the **attic** of La Pedrera. Thirteen separate apartments were built, some with raised storage cupboards according to the height of the ceiling arches. Despite being an example of the quality of 1950s design —he designed all the furnishings and fittings himself— the arches were disfigured and the building's magnificent original attic was lost.

Gaudí combined two building processes. He placed pillars and iron girders on all floors; in this way he gained the freedom to distribute the space as he wished. In the attic, on the other hand, he relied on parabolic arches to support the roof; 270 to be exact, which avoided placing too much weight on the building.

This is perhaps the most spectacular part of the building, especially when we consider that it was originally designed for a rather ordinary purpose —washing and hanging out clothes. For this reason the materials used were low-cost. The structure of parabolic arches and brick vaults turns this area into a kind of labyrinth, made all the more amazing by the different heights and thicknesses of the arches. In order to achieve greater solidity in the structure, Gaudí joined the arches at the top by means of a longitudinal axis which brings to mind a ribcage. The attic was enclosed by means of brick partitions, creating lofts which leave a perimeter walkway between them and the facade (a mediaeval evocation seen in other buildings like Bellesguard). There are four small parabolic cupolas covered with *trencadís*, situated at each corner of the facade. The windows allow for ventilation and illumination. The peculiar "canopies" give indirect light and protection from the rain.

Both entrances converge on a central ramp which leads to the **basement** in order to park vehicles, a very novel concept at that time. The structural solution proposed is remarkable. The floor of the Passeig de Gràcia courtyard rests upon a circular structure —rather like a parasol— formed by a metallic central ring from which pairs of girders emerge, like the spokes of a wheel, and meet at several points around the outer perimeter.

Perimeter walkway.

The **Espai Gaudí** is the result of a process begun in 1986 after the purchase of the building by the Caixa de Catalunya. After long and careful restoration under the direction of the architect Francisco Javier Asarta, it was inaugurated in 1996. Using the attic and the rooftop of La Pedrera, it aims to explain Gaudí's life in its historical and cultural context, and help us to understand his work by analyzing his technical innovations, in rigorous yet educational style.

In the **rooftop** Gaudí's boundless imagination fashioned one of the most fascinating roofs in twentieth-century architecture. Its aim: to create a work of art out of the normally ugly rooftop features in Barcelona.

There are six **stairwells**. They are made up of vaults in the form of truncated cones and house spiral staircases leading from the attic to the terrace. In the four nearest Passeig de Gràcia he used *trencadís* in a shade of white. The remaining two are merely plastered.

On the tops we can see Greek crosses, typical features crowning Gaudí's buildings. The stairwells have two more purposes: to ventilate the attic and to house water tanks at the top.

The **ventilation shafts** are made of double-threaded brick vaults. They take on mysterious shapes. Was it nature or the abstract that inspired them?

The **chimneys** are made of brick vaults. They can be free-standing, or arranged in groups of three or four.

At the top they turn on their own axis as if following the movement of the smoke.

The **colour scheme** keeps to a range of restrained tones both in the smooth colours used in the *trencadís* pieces —whites, yellows, beiges, blues— and in the general plasterwork in the railings and courtyards.

The **undulation of the roof** reflects the differing heights of the arches in the attic.

This is the only chimney covered with pieces of glass from bottles, and we can tell at a glance that they came from cava bottles. This material allowed him to make the feature impermeable.

The **back façade** is far more restrained than the front, but no less interesting for that. Cut stone is replaced by reddish plaster. The sinuosity is still evident. Wrought-iron bars forming a net but wound like a helix are a constant feature of this façade.

They are the most-photographed chimneys in the history of architecture. Their enigmatic forms have suggested numerous interpretations from the figures of warriors to simple sculptures.

Before the various rooftop features were made, Gaudí and the sculptor Bertran made plaster models at a scale of 1 : 10.

SAGRADA FAMÍLIA

1883-1926

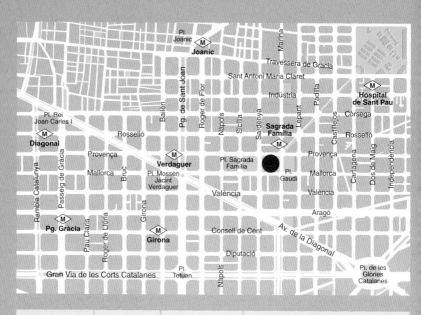

| Plaça de la Sagrada Família, s/n | **Metro** Sagrada Família | **Buses** 19, 33, 34, 43, 44, 48, 50, 51 | **Open to the public**. The temple is open daily 10am – 1.45pm and 3pm – 6pm. The crypt is open Monday to Friday 9am – 10am and 7pm – 9pm. Saturdays, 9am – 10am and 6.30pm to 8.30pm. Sundays and public holidays, 8.30am – 2pm and 6pm – 9pm. |

A way from the bourgeois residential centre of L'Eixample and on the edges of the orthogonal outline designed by Ildefons Cerdà, the area where the Sagrada Família and the parish schools stand was originally little more than fields and with only a few incipient buildings. The homogeneity set forth by the Cerdà plan regarding the building and distribution of facilities in the urban setting was in this part of the city disrupted by the construction of the great Expiatory Temple of the Holy Family —erected in spite of the fact that the site had been originally set aside for a public park— and by the extensive premises of the Hospital de la Santa Creu i de Sant Pau, by the architect Domènech i Montaner. In 1905, based on Jaussely's town plan, Gaudí proposed a project for landscaping the surroundings of the Sagrada Família, and in 1916 a plan for a star-shaped square which allowed for the minimum distances necessary to observe the temple. Although none of the projects was ever carried out, the line marked by the hospital and Gaudí's church heightens the monumental effect of the whole.

On October 3rd 1883, Gaudí accepted the commission to continue the church begun by Francisco de Paula del Villar based on an idea by Josep Mª Bocabella, founder of the *Associació Espiritual de Devots de Sant Josep* (Spiritual Association of Devotees of Saint Joseph). The church was to be dedicated to Saint Joseph and the Holy Family and was to serve as a centre for spreading the Catholic faith; its monumental size would contribute to this. He was to devote 43 years to the task. although only exclusively in the last fifteen. Such was his dedication that he even moved to the temple's workshop-studio and actively participated in fund-raising campaigns for the building. When Gaudí took over the direction of the job, part of the crypt was already built; he was to make a noticeable mark on the project.

The Sagrada Família shows both Gaudí's great mastery when it came to proposing structures, influenced by the knowledge of Gothic architecture and popular Catalan architecture, and his profound link with Christian symbolism and liturgy.

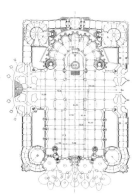

Layout of the church according to Gaudí's original plans.

Cloisters enclosing the constructions of the church (based on the original Latin meaning of *claudere*: to enclose) although, according to our concept, it should be taken to mean an external ambulatory. It is now a very small space.

Apse with ambulatory.

Crossing with nave and two aisles.

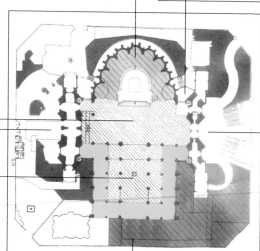

Passion and Death façade.

Nativity façade; the only one that Gaudí saw finished.

Basilical floor plan with nave and four aisles.

Main façade dedicated to Glory.

Gaudí placed twelve high **towers** dedicated to the apostles over the doorways —four towers over each— four more towers dedicated to the evangelists arranged around the central dome, which was to represent Jesus Christ and was to be the highest part, a tower dedicated to the Virgin Mary over the apse, as well as many lanterns and pinnacles.

Access to the **crypt** is by a staircase situated on the left of the apse. In Neo-Gothic style, it is circular with very slender ribbed vaulting and an ambulatory where there are seven chapels; facing, in a straight line there are five more chapels of which the central one is the altar.

The relief of the Holy Family by the sculptor Josep Llimona presides the chapel. The altar stands between the Virgin of Montserrat, patron saint of Catalonia, and Christ on the cross.

Made by Joan Flotats, the central polychrome relief aims to underline the importance of the theme of the Incarnation to the Catholic Church.

The chapel of Saint Joseph is in the centre of the ambulatory heightening the figure of the Virgin Mary's husband. The angles supporting the columns are inspired, possibly, by the tradition claiming that the angels carried the house where the Virgin Mary received the news of her conception by the Holy Ghost to Loreto (Italy).

The chapels of the ambulatory are dedicated to the Immaculate Conception, the Sacred Heart and to relatives of Jesus.

Gaudí, a great devotee of the Virgin of Carmen, chose to be buried in her chapel. The tomb is covered with a simple tombstone where his birthplace in Reus and his work as the architect of the temple is inscribed in Latin.

The **apse** was finished in 1893. It is clearly Neo-Gothic in style, although one may observe naturalistic motifs. Gaudí claimed that it was an improvement on the Gothic style.

According to Gothic tradition, the gargoyles represent animals related with evil: frogs, lizards, snakes...which might mean the expulsion of negativity from the Lord's house.

On the pinnacles we can see floral motifs and distinguish ears of corn related in Christian liturgy with the Eucharist and, therefore, with Christ.

The **Rosary Chapel** is one of the chapels that were to be situated at the angles of the cloisters and the only one designed by Gaudí. It recreates Flamboyant Gothic with a profusion of ornamentation.

The Virgin of the Rosary appears inside an ogival frame surrounded by a sculptural explosion of flowers and geometric patterns. She is flanked by Saint Dominic and Saint Catherine of Sienna.

The dome seen from below.

The **temptations**: These reliefs represent the dangers of the temptation by evil. Thus, we may observe how a woman is tempted by a monster in the form of a fish, which offers her a bag of money, and a man with a bomb in his hand —at the turn of the century attacks carried out by anarchist groups were frequent. Nevertheless, both overcome the temptation by offering themselves to the Virgin, as the direction of their gaze indicates.

The **Nativity façade** was the first one finished. Work on it lasted from 1891 to 1900. It comprises three doors, dedicated to the theological virtues of Faith, Hope and Charity. The middle door is the largest. The façade is completed by four towers. Their spectacular sculpture work, expressionist, baroque, naturalist and imbued with a profound religious spirit tries to show the main dogma of Catholicism in a pedagogical fashion and explain the events surrounding Christ's birth and infancy. The majority of the sculptures were done by Joan Matamala. The far simpler inside of the façade contrasts with the profusion outside.

The Faith Doorway

The Visitation of Mary to her cousin Saint Elizabeth after the announcement of her conception by the Holy Ghost.

Jesus arguing with the Pharisees about the Fait

The presentation of Jesus in the Temple. This sculpture is crowned by a relief featuring ears of corn and grapes, symbols of the Eucharist. It is framed by a relief in the form of a grotto, very usual in garden decoration at the end of the 19th century; the natural elements fuse with the sacred referring back to pre-Christian religions.

Symbol of the Trinity formed by a three-armed lamp; above appears the Immaculate Conception, a dogma of faith proclaimed by the Church in 1854. Above this is the hand with the eye of God symbolizing Providence.

Jesus in the carpenter's workshop.

Gargoyle in the form of a chameleon.

The Hope Doorway

The flight to Egypt.

Saw symbolizing Saint Joseph with the M for Mary.

Gargoyle in the form of a chameleon.

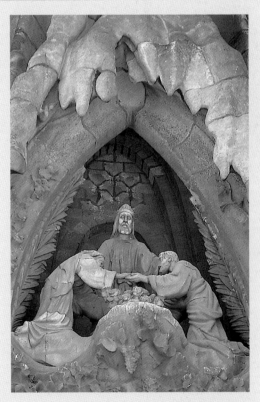

Saint Joseph and Jesus with his grandparents; we see many tools belonging to Saint Joseph's trade.

nt Joseph, patron saint of the Church, ling the ship that symbolizes the titution.

The nuptials of the Virgin and Saint Joseph framed in a relief in the form of a grotto.

e slaughter of the Innocents.

The Charity Doorway

The coronation of the Virgin.

The Annunciatio
by the Archang
Gabriel to Mary
her conception b
the Holy Ghost.

The columns flanking the central door represent the Virgin and Saint Joseph, as we can read in the in scriptions situated halfway up. The top halves of the columns feature palm leaves and above them are angels who, with their trumpets, announce the Last Judgement. On the bases we can see two tortoises symbolizing longevity and therefore, the durability of the Church.

symbol of Jesus.

The adoration of the shepherds.

The birth of Jesus, the chief element in the centre of the facade; the ox and the donkey can also be seen.

The adoration of the Magi.

Polychrome ceramic cypress made after 1926. Gaudí chose as his model an example from the Charterhouse of Montalegre in Tiana (Barcelona). This tree symbolizes eternity and life. We can see numerous doves, a symbol linked to the origins of Christianity. The cypress is crowned with a T, the initial of the Greek word for God.

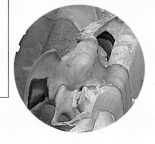

Figure of the pelican, symbolizing Charity.

The trunk of a palm tree symbolizing Christ's family tree, as the names of his ancestors appear written.

We also see the serpent with the apple of sin, the reason why Christ came into the world.

Angels with musical instruments.

Group of angels announcing the good tidings.

The four **bell towers** of the Nativity façade are dedicated to Saint Barnabus, Saint Simon, Saint Judas Thaddeus and Saint Matthias. The exterior ones are 94 metres high and the interior ones are 107 metres. They constitute a geometry lesson in themselves and have a complex structure. They start with a square-shaped base that changes to circular at the level of the two small side balconies. They continue cylindrically before becoming parabolic (externally defined by the longitudinal openings). The purpose of the stone baffles was to better distribute the sound of the bells.

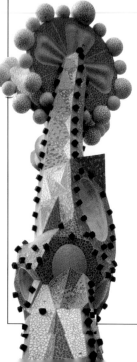

Building work on the Saint Barnabus tower, the only one Gaudí saw finished before his death.

Detail of the ornamentation on the top of the towers: rosettes made from *trencadís*.

The tops of the towers, 25 metres high, represent the bishops whose attributes are shown: ring, crosier, mitre and cross. The words Hosanna Excelsis can be made out on hexagonal pieces. They are covered in Murano glass due to its greater resistance to inclement weather.

The optical effect of the spiral staircases at the bottom is fascinating. They do not turn in the same direction, as the twin towers have different twists.

After Gaudí

After Gaudí's death in 1926, the project was continued by
the architects Domènech Sugrañes and Francesc de Paula
Quintana until the towers on the Nativity façade were finished. During the Civil War many of the original drawings
were lost in a fire in the workshop. In 1954 the work was
begun again by Isidre Puig Boada and Lluís Bonet Garí, among other architects. The four bell
towers on the Passion façade were finished in 1976. In 1985 Jordi Bonet was appointed as
works director. Since 1988 Josep Mª Subirachs has been working on the sculptures on the
Passion façade.

The continuity of the
work has been and still is
the subject of controver-
sy, as the question has
been raised as to whether
it is possible to be faithful
to Gaudí's ideas after
almost all the documenta-
tion has been lost. More-
over, Gaudí exercised
constant control over the
work, modifying and
innovating as the building
process advanced.

Although formally the same scheme imagined by Gaudí has
been followed, it is evident that the execution is notably different from the Gaudinian figures. Subirachs is trying to recreate
Passion and Death with a tragic schematism.

Basing himself on some fragmentary sources, remains of the models and a few photographs, and applying a computerised treatment to the geometric forms observed, Jordi Bonet and his team postulate that there is an underlying modulation in Gaudí's architectural structures in the Sagrada Família. The continuation of the work on the temple has been decided based on the study of numerical series that are repeated in the structures, where the multiples and divisors of twelve are present.

The basis of Gaudí's architecture is the observation of nature as expressed in geometry. We can see this in the great columns of the nave which, starting with a square base, become circular towards the top, branching out into two, three or five columns after the knot, as if they were trees.

Brick-lined vaults used to cover the central nave at a height of 45 metres; they are decorated with palm leaves and end in hyperboloidal shapes. Above them a dome rises to a height of 170 metres, making the Sagrada Família the highest building in Barcelona (now superseded by the twin towers in the Vila Olímpica). Columns made of porphyry, a material originally from Iran and considered to be the most durable stone of all, rise in the apse and transept.

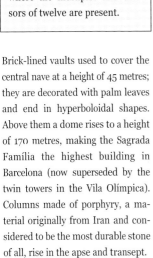

The Parish Schools

These schools, whilst waiting to be installed near the cloisters of the Church of the Sagrada Família, were provisionally built in the area of the Glory façade between 1909 and 1910. It seems that Gaudí took his inspiration from the houses used by Mediterranean fisherman to keep their boats in. Although covering only 200 square metres this apparently humble building served Gaudí's purpose in his experiment to come up with a constructional solution that impressed even Le Corbusier on his visit to Barcelona in 1928.

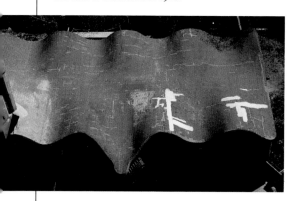

Notes made by Le Corbusier on his visit to the schools.

The building features sinuous forms both in the walls and the roof. The three classrooms contained inside were enclosed by sloping walls of solid brickwork supporting a brick roof made up of a series of conical surfaces which form the alternating undulation we can see.

With this system Gaudí achieved the maximum resistance and stability with the minimum amount of material. In Gaudí's lifetime this roof, laid on a series of wooden rafters supported by a horizontal iron girder, was visible; after the restoration carried out after the Civil war of 1936, ceilings were put in which hide this structure.

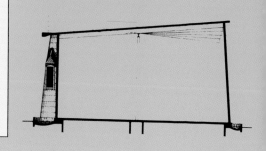

The classroom furniture, designed personally by Gaudí, was totally functional and adapted to the pupils' needs: desks, three-legged stools, gyrating cupboards and marvellous lavatories with the most up-to-date features of the time.

There is a playground for each classroom with a capacity for 44, 50 and 56 pupils respectively —named the Puríssima, the Angel and the Sacred Heart. In each one there was a sun shade made of heather where classes were conducted outside. Also, along the perimeter of the playground there was a small garden where the pupils planted and tended flowers.

In 1934 and 1939 the schools suffered fires causing irreparable damage. They were successively rebuilt by the architects Domènec Sugrañes and Francesc de Paula Quintana with noticeable modifications.

GAUDI'S WORK IN SPAIN

EL CAPRICHO
(1883-1885) - Comillas (Santander)

This summer villa built for the Marquis of Comillas' brother-in-law is a building with an irregular shape and a sloping roof corresponding to Gaudí's early period, in which the oriental influence is very evident. Whilst it does not produce any structural innovation, it deserves & mention for its surprising ornamental work using textures and materials that give the building great vivacity. The facade combines ceramics, brickwork of an ochre tone perfectly in keeping with the natural surroundings and light-coloured sandstone for the skirting board. Characteristic of the building is the horizontal feel conferred upon it by the ornamental strips, compensated by the cylindrical tower covered in green ceramic tiling resting on a four-columned rotunda. Noteworthy is the join between the roof and the facade, using cartouches made of bricks placed in stepped form.

EPISCOPAL PALACE
(1887-1893) - Astorga (León)

Commissioned by the Junta Diocesana de Templos de Astorga, it belongs to Gaudí's Gothic-historicist period, recreating a mediaeval castle. It was continued by other architects, who introduced changes to the roof with respect to the original project. Starting with a square ground plan, Gaudí compensates this powerful geometrical layout by adding four towers with cylindrical vertices and prolonging it with several parts —throne room, chapel, library and reception room. The building is organized around a central space where the architect experiments with the entry of light, a recurring theme throughout his career. The exterior facade is made up of granite stone blocks giving it a solid, sober appearance. In the interior he creates spaces by using capitals, cross-ribbed vaulting and Gothic-style ogival arches.

CASA DE LOS BOTINES

(1891-1892) León

This residential building also belongs to Gaudí's early period, characterized by the statement of historicist themes: once again Gothic is his source of inspiration. Its compact appearance brings to mind a mediaeval castle and indeed he recreates one, even going so far as to surround the building with a moat protected by railings at the entrance. Approximately rectangular in shape, the building has cylindrical towers resting on corbels and crowned with slate roofed conical spires, one at each corner. The facade is of limestone blocks with Gothic-style slits. The Casa de los Botines is the civil replica of the Episcopal Palace of Astorga.